FACE
LANGUAGE

Library of Congress Cataloging-in-Publication Data

Whiteside, Robert L.
    Face Language / by Robert Whiteside.
       p. cm.
    Rev. ed. of: Face Language, 1974.
    ISBN 0-8119-0763-5 : $9.95
    1. Physiognomy, 2. Facial expression. I. Whiteside, Robert L.
Face Language. II. Title.
BF851.W55   1992   92-14189
138—dc20   CIP

Manufactured in the United States of America
1 2 3 4 5 6 7 8 9 0

FACE LANGUAGE

By Robert L. Whiteside

A Guide
To Meeting
The Right Person...

LIFETIME BOOKS, INC.
Hollywood, Florida

People with live eyes lead lively lives. Here's someone who is vivacious and sparkly. She is also open-minded, energetic, and has an idealistic swing. But, she has a modest opinion of herself in spite of all her abilities.

ACKNOWLEDGEMENTS

In the creation of this book, I want particularly to acknowledge the artists who have shared their talents: John W. Grossman, twice chairman of the California State Art Commission and creator of the personology logo; Opal Page, gifted Independence, Mo. artist; Vivienne Barrett, the versatile Californian who also did the illustrations for my "Animal Language" book; Christine Cummins of Phoenix, Arizona; and Claudia Rompel of Frankfurt, West Germany.

I also wish to thank Jack Williamson of Honolulu, Hawaii, for magnanimously furnishing pictures from his huge number showing that these human qualities apply to all races. Tom Brown of Phoenix and others deserve appreciation for their assistance with photographs; and numerous other people who assisted in various ways. Appreciation goes to my wife, Marion, for her help in so many areas.

And, I appreciate the encouragement and urging so many people have given me to produce a new, updated "Face Language" now that the original best-sellers are completely sold out.

Robert L. Whiteside
Maui, Hawaii, 1992

INTRODUCTION
(By the author)

This book provides you with a quick-reference handbook to face language.

The main reason for this book is that my original bestsellers "Face Language," and "Face Language II" are sold out after a number of printings. And, there is a widespread demand, including request for more comprehensive treatment, to include traits not included in the introductory volume.

Face language and the biological approach are so much the "in" thing now, that the introductory bestseller was reproduced in many foreign languages — including Japanese, Hebrew and Norweigian — and became required reading at one time in three courses in the United States Air Force Academy.

Brain research has demonstrated more and more how much of our nature stems from our physical build. (A spin-off from this research that is popular is the "right brain/left brain" knowledge.)

Even more dramatic are the findings of studies involving the reunion of identical twins (and triplets) raised in different environments.

A SPECIAL NOTE

This guide to face language has to do primarily with how the structure of the face indicates a person's disposition.

Momentary expressions, of course, are valuable to notice too. But they require no special instruction to understand. You have a rich reservoir of memory of all kinds of expressions: love, hate; joy, sorrow; fun, seriousness; pleasure, pain; relaxation, hurry; concentration, impatience; ecstasy, despair; mischief, stolidity; flirting, dislike; and dozens of others. You need no coaching to recognize these. But, you have found you DO need coaching on how to best deal with them.

Noticing these expressions tips you off to how the other person is feeling at the moment, and reminds you of the situation he or she is in. But progressing from there and DEALING with that human being, requires you to proceed according to that human being's own UNIQUE build. "What is one man's meat is another's poison."

For example, if they have large eyes, they are affectionate, and your TONE OF VOICE means everything to them. But, if they have tight, thin lips, keep it brief. Don't rattle on, or you will spoil the gain you have made.

You will find this face-language guide a valuable book for teaching you HOW TO deal specifically with others most important to you, in the specific actions of REAL DAILY LIFE.

HOW MUCH OF YOU IS JUST NATURALLY YOU?

How much of you is just naturally you — born in you (nature) — and how much of you is a result of the environment (nurture)?

Most of what makes you the distinct, unique individual that you are, was born into you. The same goes for others with whom you deal.

So has been the report of Dr. Thomas J. Bouchard of the University of Minnesota. Dr. Bouchard headed a team that studied genetically identical twins who had been separated at birth, raised in different homes and reunited as adults.

Take, for example, the "Jim Twins" of Ohio. Newborn, they were adopted by families in different communities. Grown, they found each other at a small beach in Florida that they both preferred. They discovered:

*Each had married a girl named Betty and divorced her, then married a woman named Linda to whom he is still married. Both leave mash notes around the house.

*Each drives a Chevrolet, drinks Miller Light, and smokes the same brand of cigarette.

*Each lives in the only house on a block that has a tree. Each has a hobby of woodwork and has built a wooden bench around his tree.

*Each has the same history of migraines, weight gain and weight loss. Each has hemorrhoids.

*Each has had a pet dog named Toy.

*Each has been in law enforcement. And, each is behind in his loan payments.

These are the kinds of things people do if they have the same genetic coding.

Dr. Bouchard reported on "The Phil Donahue Show" that one's interests, personality, style of movement and expression, and general abilities, are all determined more by genetics than by environment.

The next question you naturally ask is, "If that much of our individual nature is carried around in our build, what are the indicators? How do we know what to look for?"

That is what this book is all about. So read ahead for the specifics. You will find that the physical indicators are natural and logical. The function goes with the structure: "isomorhic." Verbal expression factors are found more in the mouth area, judgement factors in and about the eyes, etc.

Even our language is biological:

"Thin-skinned" — "Thick-skinned"

"Tight-mouthed" — "Mouthy"

"Soft, wishy-washy" — "Hard, tough"

"Narrow-minded" — "Broad-minded"

"Sharp" — "Blunt"

"Level-headed" — "Knuckle-headed"

"Tied in knots"

"Nosey"

"Sourpuss"

"High Brow"

"Leads with his chin"

These are three ways in which traits are indicated:

1. Proportions of specialized cells within the person
2. Indications of current functioning (such as worry lines)
3. Genetic syndromes (outward "tip of the iceberg" traits)

This guide to face language concentrates on the basic disposition of the individual, as evidenced by the individual's own unique structure. In enables you to predict behavior, to a degree. It is fundamental, and tells you the constitutional "hot buttons" to press. It does not concern itself with the more fleeting facial expressions. They are a separate subject.

This book is arranged in a practical reference form to make it easy for you to size up other people and deal more effectively with them.

And, it equips you, for the first time, with a specific PROCESS for dealing with each person as an individual (instead of generalizing) in your daily life.

DEDICATION

To my wife and helpmate, Marion

WHAT'S IN A FACE?

"Why do faces fascinate you?"

"Why do you study them?"

"Because there's so much in them to understand, once you know the language. Some of it you know almost instinctively, because the right side of your brain has stored up and recorded thousands of faces. But to consciously understand the knowledge the other person's face provides for you, this book is your guide."

Why do you study faces? You sense how much is there — how much those faces can tell you if you know the "language." This book gives you the "alphabet" for reading people. It includes 20 traits more than its bestselling predecessor, "Face Language."

TRAITS EXIST IN ALL RACES

It's the same in all races . . .
The native qualities which make us human beings . . .
And it is shown in our build, but . . .
Best of all, in our FACE

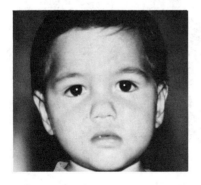 

TABLE OF CONTENTS

TRAITS BY AREAS

What do the traits here tell you?
A strong nature balanced by a
love of beauty and music, and a
gift for words and their flow.

The warm expression you get
from this face comes from the
large eyes, the friendly eyebrows
and the full, generous lips.

Note the oral-expression talent
of this man, along with his all-
around leadership abilities. The
combination of ideals with his
objective and administrative
side give balance to his nature.
And, you can depend on him to
take care of the details too.

The creative, friendly and helpful traits are all high with this
young lady. Of course, she is
attractive, but if you will start
looking trait-wise, you will also
that she is highly intelligent.

Notice the dramatic flair here? This is someone who has a sense of the theatrical, can act quite different roles, and knows just how to make entrances and exits to effect. The upward arch of the eyebrows is, of course, the key to her dramatic side, but if you will observe the eyes themselves, you will notice that she is a perfectionist and could supervise or coach.

The trait of physical insulation is important to know about, whether you live in balmy Hawaii (as in the upper picture), or in a more rigorous climate, as illustrated in the lower photograph.

One
Eye-Area Traits

Narrow-set eyes, low tolerance

Quickly indignant

Tolerance, low

Unconcerned, high tolerance

High tolerance

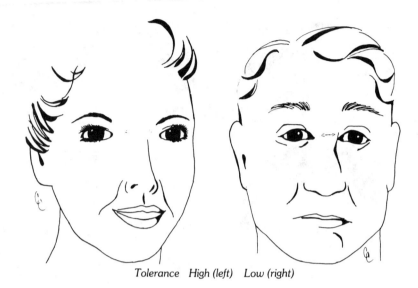

Tolerance   High (left)   Low (right)

TOLERANCE

If you look in the dictionary, you will see that many words have a variety of meanings, depending on how they are used.

For the word "tolerance," my standard encyclopedia dictionary has five definitions:

1. The character, state or quality of being tolerant.
2. Freedom from bigotry or from racial or religious prejudice.
3. The act of enduring, or the capacity for endurance.
4. A small permissible allowance for variations from the specified weight, dimensions, etc.
5. (Medicine) Ability to tolerate, as a drug.

Definition four is the kind of tolerance meant in personology — the deviation from perfection that will be allowed. It is NOT racial or religious tolerance.

The physical indication for this trait is the relative space between the eyes. The farther apart the eyes are set, the broader the view. The closer the eyes are together, the closer the view. This is another isomorphic trait, the function following the structure: "iso" meaning the same and "morph" meaning form.

The man or woman with eyes set noticeably far apart will tolerate more before saying "that does it!" and putting their foot down. They are more easygoing and more companionable, but inclined to procrastinate and let situations build up or get out of hand. They are good sports (spelled s-u-c-k-e-r) and are easily taken advantage of. They mean well, but are inclined only to really perform when things get late enough or bad enough. They are always and forever "in the doghouse" for actions or situations where they INTENDED no wrong, but which they did permit to develop. They often get misinterpreted as being lazy. They are good-natured and seldom ulcer-prone.

The reverse build has the reverse characteristics. You will notice that people who are noticeably close between the eyes take a closer, more concerned view, and are perfectionists. They get upset more quickly when they see something that is not the way it should be, and they want it made right, IMMEDIATELY. Like the great tennis player John McEnroe, not only do they become upset at seeing what others do not appear to be doing right, they get upset at themselves when they are not performing perfectly. They do a great job, but are extremely hard on themselves. They get misunderstood as being narrow, always complaining, and impossible to please, when they are really just trying to have things right. It is a big relief to them when they realize they are responsible only for their own performance and can stop trying to carry the whole world on their shoulders.

In between these two extremes are the people who have a "just tolerance." They are strict enough to get things done, but broad enough to see both sides of the matter. They simply do what is to be done, without either putting it off or complaining. They are fair and equitable. They make great judges or referees. Their physical indicator is that the eyes are evenly placed, neither on the narrow side nor the broad side. The overly tolerant people regard them as too strict, and the narrow-tolerance people regard them as not strict enough.

What to do around those with broad tolerance:

1. Expect tardiness and easygoing performance
2. Set deadlines and give reminders.
3. Enjoy their good-natured, easy-to-please company.

What to do around someone with narrower tolerance:

1. Be careful of your performance and statements.
2. Be on time.
3. Expect indignation and over-reaction.
4. Trust them with things that have to be done right, and put them in a supervisory position, if possible.

Around those with just-tolerance, you can relax — and, if you desire to know the fair thing to do about something, ask them.

    *   *   *   *   *

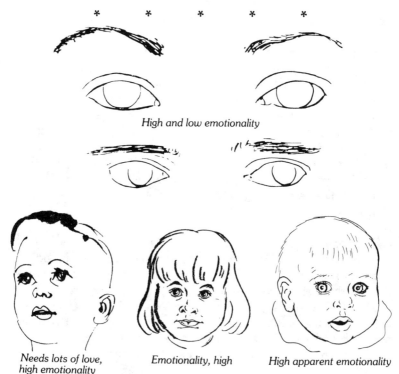

High and low emotionality

Needs lots of love,
high emotionality   *Emotionality, high*   *High apparent emotionality*

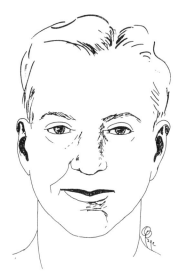

Low emotionality

Emotionality, low

Apparent emotionality

EMOTIONALITY AND AFFECTIONATENESS

If you want someone who will be affectionate, choose a person with large, warm eyes. If you want someone who will be matter-of-fact and businesslike, pick a person with small, beady eyes. (This is applicable also in the animal kingdom, such as in choosing pets — the lap-dog or loving cocker spaniel have relatively large eyes.)

Every human being has feelings, but the large-eyed people express their feelings more openly. They are more demonstrative and exhibit more charisma. They laugh more. They hug, wink and cuddle. They cheer and jeer at games, and give ovations at the opera. They cry at movies and even at weddings. They make decisions in business on the basis of friendship or love, unless other, more prudent, traits are sufficient to hold them back.

If you are hiring a bill collector, select someone with small, cool, matter-of-fact eyes. He or she will get the job done as ordinary routine, instead of "bleeding in their shoes" at the sight of the debtor's suffering and humiliation.

There is a time and a place where each trait can be valuable. A surgeon should not let emotions distract him. Because of the power of this trait, if possible, he should avoid operating on any member of his own family.

You can make your own application as to where affectionateness fits into lovemaking. For the affectionate one, being LOVED comes first, and the physical aspects follow as the a la mode.

There are feelings inside the less demonstrative individual too, but the actions can appear to be strictly biological. I recall a preacher who referred his wife to counseling because in the most intimate phase of marriage, she would blandly crunch an apple, her mind on other things (a sure way to deflate the husband's manly pride).

What to remember around the emotional person:

1. They take everything as an indication of whether or not you like them. Keep the expression on your face smiling and friendly, and your tone of voice companionable.

2. Break bread with them. Say, "let's have lunch together and talk it over." Talk about mutual friends and how they are doing, the children, and old times.

3. Call them up if you're in their town. Bring gifts to the hostess. Remember their birthdays and anniversaries. Stand up and give a toast to them at their dinner party.

When with someone whose feelings are more buried:

1. Bear in mind that their feelings are the same as anyone else's, just more deeply buried. "There's gold in them thar hills." Keep digging, and you can bring it out.

2. Expect less evident jubilation or despair. Give them credit for what they do show.

3. In a business session, be well-prepared and stick to the subject. Leave out talk about feelings or family. Anticipate a briefer session and always put business before pleasure.

*   *   *   *   *

Critical perception,   *Less critical*   *Critical perception, low*
finds the flaws

CRITICAL PERCEPTION

The trait of criticalness is a prime example that no human quality is good or bad except as it is used. Critical perception spots the flaw, and possibly could have saved the space shuttle from exploding. But, being wrongly critical has broken up many a marriage — the spouse on the receiving end finally gets fed up and decides to not take it any more.

Criticalness is indicated structurally by the eye slanting downward toward the outer corner. This is the person who notices anything out of line — such as the load not tied on sufficiently that will fall off when the first corner is turned. This is the inspector, the auditor, the detective, the coach, the quarterback, the editor, the proofreader and the one naturally good at target sports.

Mr. or Ms. Critical can also see advantages and opportunities, and usually end up well-to-do. They are usually put in charge of other people because of their ability to see first what needs to be done. What they need to be careful of is unnecessary criticism in personal relationships; such as losing a friend by pointing out that he or she ought to do something about his or her dandruff.

In contrast, the individual whose eyes slant up to the outside away from the nose is not as critical. He or she is the opposite of the nagger or fault-finder. They are easier to be with, but often encounter difficulties by failing to notice flaws or opportunities.

What to do around the critical individual:

1. Get their advice when you need it. (They will be GLAD to give it.)
2. Don't be hurt by unsolicited criticism. Remember that they're just built that way — it has nothing to do with whether they love or like you. Keep in mind that underneath they have a heart of gold.
3. Try to take care of things that involve them in order to avoid their criticism.

What to do around the non-critical individual:

1. Don't trust their advice or evaluations too much.
2. Enjoy their failure to point out your insufficiencies (most of which you are probably already aware of anyway).
3. Include them in your social gatherings.

       *   *   *   *   *

Not stubborn — just analytical

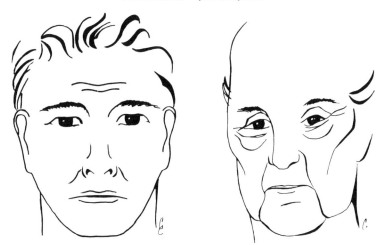

Analytical (left) Less analytical (right)

Low analyticalness

ANALYTICALNESS

Look at your folding money. The upper eyelid is covered on the picture of Alexander Hamilton, who analyzed so well in setting up the U.S. Treasury Department that it is still functioning in spite of modern financial gymnastics. But, the upper eyelid is plainly visible on Andrew Jackson's picture. Jackson was a direct-actionist who had a pirate assisting him in his defeat of the British in the hurry-up Battle of New Orleans.

The analytical man or woman frequently is misinterpreted as stubborn because he or she won't say yes, no or maybe until they have found out what it is all about — why it has to be done, and why it has to be done THAT way. But, they are great at figuring things out and at helping others to understand cause and effect.

The less analytical, direct-actionist cuts through and does the obvious with less cross-examination. He or she makes a good paramedic — they jump in and get the injured out of a crashed vehicle before it blows up, rather than wondering how in the world a van could have gotten upset like that at a 15-mile-an-hour intersection.

What to do when with the analytical person:

1. Tell them the set up before you ask them to do it.
2. Remember, you only need to explain it to them once.
3. Ask them to figure something out for you or explain to you the hows and whys (they will love doing it).

What to do when with the direct-actionist:

1. Don't irritate them with lengthy explanations.
2. Expect swift, direct action
3. Anticipate a cool quality in the way they cut through and get things done (although, to some, it may seem ruthless at times).

*   *   *   *   *

Magnetism

Magnetism, "stars in the eyes"

Magnetism

MAGNETISM

Think of people you know. Those with bright, sparkly eyes are the ones who attract everyone. They are animated and full of spirit. (Horsemen choose their horses partly for this same characteristic.)

People with dull eyes tend to lead dull lives and are less fun to be around.

Fortunately, this is a trait that can be cultivated. Look in the mirror and think of what you most love — your eyes will brighten. In a way, magnetism or charm is spirit shining out. The eyes are indeed the "windows to the soul."

Unfortunately, those of you with charm or magnetism must keep your other traits in hand and take care of yourself. If you have missed sleep or meals and are exhausted, the charisma ebbs. Likewise, if you have an unsettled problem on your mind and a troubled look in your eye.

What to do around someone with a lot of magnetism and charm:

1. Invite them to your parties; they'll brighten them up.
2. Hire or appoint them to places in your scheme of things. They have a gift of getting their way with people.
3. Expect other people to be attracted to them.

What to do around someone lacking magnetism and charm:

1. Be glad it's them instead of you.
2. Bring along a good book.
3. Remember that you can brighten them up if you get them to talk about their hobby or something they enjoy.

Serious-minded, takes a serious view

SERIOUS-MINDEDNESS

There is a law of rhythm in life, but the serious-minded people, those with deep-set eyes, always seem to be on the serious side. They take themselves seriously. They also take their responsibilities seriously. Other people sense this and tend to give them responsibilities beyond their age. They take life seriously. They enjoy humor more than they produce it.

The people whose eyes are not deep-set are more free-wheeling, lively and have a more settled-back mental attitude. All in all, they are more lighthearted, and shift more easily into a holiday mood.

If you are dealing with someone who is serious-minded:

1. Don't expect outbursts of humor but know that he or she is probably enjoying it more than is visibly apparent.

2. Give them serious tasks.
3. Appeal to his or her sense of responsibility.

If you are dealing with someone less serious-minded:

1. Your jokes will get a more open response.
2. You can talk about lighter subjects.
3. You have more freedom in behavior; things you do won't be taken as seriously.

Fugacity — "all upset"

Fugacity

FUGACITY

When you see someone with glassy eyes, it usually indicates that the person is under pressure and uptight. The eyes may also be bloodshot. The skin and eyes are dry and shiny.

Our term for this outward evidence of feeling under pressure is "fugacity," which comes from the same root word as fugitive. It means that the person feels "on the run."

The opposite, complete peace and relaxation, is best illustrated by the clear, moist eyes of a baby when it wakes up after a pleasant afternoon nap. The whites of the eyes are very white, and there are little beads of moisture on the eyelids.

A person's eyes are so intimately connected with the brain that fugacity can show in an instant; such as when you realize you have lost you wallet. But, it can also disappear just as quickly; such as when you feel in the other pocket and find you still have your wallet.

If you want to see spectacular examples of fugacity, hang out around automobile accidents, courtrooms, stock markets or airports where travelers wait at the end of a long line at the ticket counter hearing the last announcement for their plane when they haven't gotten their ticket yet. Another good example to be found at the airport is passengers arriving sleepless on the overnight "red-eye" plane.

In any case, when you see glassy eyes, you know that the man, woman or child does not feel that they have their situation in hand.

What to do when with someone with "fugacity" or glassy eyes:

1. Take it easy. Remember they are under pressure and their decisions and actions are not liable to be at their best.
2. Wait until later to present a project, unless it is something that will solve their problem and take pressure off them.
3. Do what you can to help them relax. Offer them a drink of water. Be nice, quiet, good-humored and not too obtrusive.

If the person you are with does not have this trait, you can conduct business as usual.

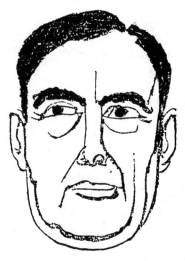

Casualty syndrome — accident prone

CASUALTY TREND

Some connection has been noted between one eye pointing higher than the other and the individual's proneness to accidents.

Having reached the age of 80 last year, I'm still on this planet because I found out that I was accident-prone when I had my personology (structure/function) analysis done at the age of 33. When my casualty trend was pointed out to me, I recalled car accidents that I had already experienced. I decided from then on to be religiously careful when driving. I also gave up flying (I had just soloed in training). Unfortunately, I never bothered to tell my instructor about having a personology analysis — he was killed 90 days later when his plane crashed into a hillside.

Remember that the physical indication for this trait is NOT whether one eye sits higher on the face than the other, but whether one eye POINTS higher than the other (a vertical strabismus). The eye pointing upward may even have some white showing right under the iris.

Another thing to remember is that this condition may not be so evident at all times, but rather becomes apparent when the individual is under stress.

So, what do you do when you notice a casualty trend in someone? Some suggestions:

1. Offer to do the driving.
2. Urge them to take it easy or get some rest, and encourage them to be careful around sharp equipment and hot liquids.
3. Expect breakage of dishes, etc.

This does not apply if this trait is non-existent.

*   *   .*   *   *

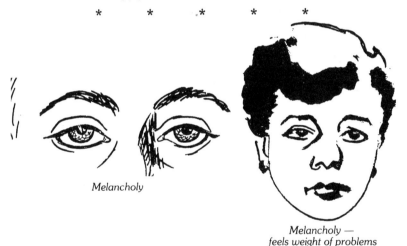

Melancholy

Melancholy —
feels weight of problems

MELANCHOLY

That sad look that eyes have when white shows under the iris indicate a sad, unresolved situation within the individual.

It may be a perfectly innocent problem, such as being plain exhausted from working double shifts to earn the money to put a child through medical school. The person is so tired he or she doesn't know whether it's Tuesday or Thursday.

Or, it may be that the person is doing something they are ashamed of, such as being on drugs or having an affair that they hope no one (especially their spouse) will find out about.

Whatever the cause, it is bad news whenever white of the sclera shows beneath the iris. When the melancholy person has a relaxing experience, such as laughing or a proper sexual experience, the indication of gloominess may go away for awhile, but inevitably it will return because of the unresolved problem that has become such a burden on the individual. It will disappear permanently only when the problem is satisfactorily resolved.

What to do when you are around someone with obvious melancholy:

1. Give them a chance to unload — this will happen more easily than you expect, especially if no one else is around. Tell them where they can go for help.
2. Don't expect genuine cheerfulness.
3. Don't hire them, or get too involved with them, until their problem is resolved; otherwise, their problem will become your problem too.

What to do when you are around someone with normal eyes, free from the indication of melancholy: not applicable, business as usual. But, there will be plenty of other traits to pay attention to.

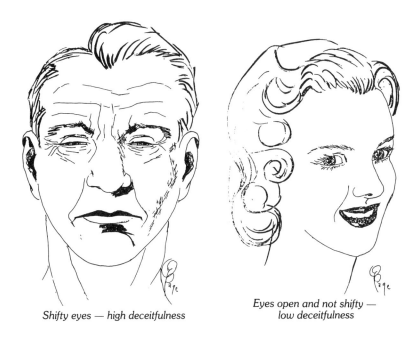

Shifty eyes — high deceitfulness

Eyes open and not shifty —
low deceitfulness

SHIFTY EYES

Once, when going through the agriculture inspection of my luggage at the Maui airport, I asked the inspector, "How do you tell when people are lying?"

"They look away," he replied.

If someone's eyes do not meet yours, it does not always mean they are deceitful. It may just mean that they are uncomfortable at your gaze, do not agree with you, or have not yet figured out what action they want to take. But, in any case, it's an unfavorable sign — you know that they are not in full open agreement. Do not expect them to carry through on anything they appear to agree with at that time. They are not in harmony with it.

The eyes are the exposed part of the nervous system which is so intimately and thoroughly interconnected. For the eyes to be well-relaxed, an inner peacefulness must exist. Dr. William Howard Hay found with the retinascope that a person's eyes will go momentarily out of focus if he or she tells even a "little white lie." For example, someone who is 24 to say they are 25.

What to do when the person you are dealing with has shifty eyes:

1. Beware. Be cautious in trusting this person.
2. Stay out of harm's way.
3. Expect no follow-through on that person's part.

What to do around someone with a clear, open, forthright gaze: realize that this is a good sign and you can conduct business as usual, at least as far as this particular trait is concerned.

Special Note: So common is the knowledge that people are going to be uneasy around you if you don't meet their gaze, some hardened individuals will meet your eye with a brazen stare when they tell a real whopper. But, you will recognize the unnaturalness of their gaze because it is a fixed, brassy gaze that does not focus on your eyes, but rather seems to look beyond you. A good example is the teenager who tells you what a tough exam he had yesterday in math when, in reality, he wasn't in class at all because he skipped school all day with his chums.

*   *   *   *   *

Discriminative

Discriminative

*Affectionate and emotional,
but discriminative*

Affable, easy to meet

Affable

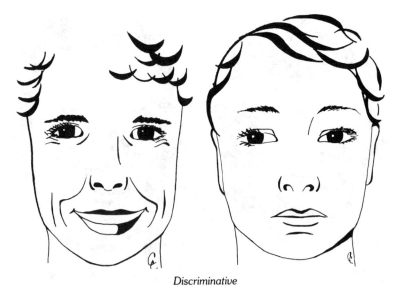

Discriminative

AFFABILITY

Some people have an easy, engaging way of meeting others and making friends. Others, appear more aloof and reserved.

If you look carefully, you will notice that affable people have eyebrows close to their eyes. Conversely, the more distant, formal people are built with eyebrows relatively high. Prototypes are Tom Selleck, type-cast as the casual, informal Magnum of "Magnum P.I.;" and John Hillerman, type-cast as the more formal Higgins who is strong on protocol and horrified at Magnum's lack of desire to move through proper channels.

There are no strangers to the affable individual. He or she has a gift of acting around new people as if they were old friends. They can sell from door to door. And, as your house guest, you can expect them to act as if they were already at home (often, not even bothering to knock).

The discriminative individual is selective in his or her belongings and friends. These people take much longer to accept someone, but, once they DO, they accept them wholeheartedly. Their style, once they have decided upon it, is all-or-nothing, no halfway.

What to do around the affable:

1. Expect and enjoy their informality.
2. Warn them about protocol.
3. Put them in greeter, host or hostess positions.

What to do when with the discriminative individual:

1. Mind your manners. Be on your best behavior. Use courtesies. Ask permission before touching personal belongings.
2. Use titles where they apply. Don't call them by their first name unless they call you by yours.
3. Remember that once you are accepted by them, the walls will come down. Also remember that they are not "stuck up," or think that they are better than you but may, in fact, be quite lonesome.

Two

Additional
Eye-Area Traits

Esthetic

ESTHETIC

You can get along better with people who have flat straight eyebrows if you remember that they are artists at heart. They feel beauty and rhythm. They want to make an art out of whatever they do, and are sure to end up very interested in some form of art, music or literature.

The esthetic person enjoys having a home with a view, waking up to music and dining to candlelight. He or she wants beauty and harmony in life. They may even make an art out of a particular sport.

There is a tendency for the esthete to geographically remove himself or herself from discord. Many men and women have left their spouse and young children because of dirty diapers and dirty dishes. Sooner or later, the esthete must learn to jump in and do his share of creating the harmony he craves, instead of expecting that a change of geography or person will take care of it for him.

What to do when dealing with the esthetic individual:

1. Be harmonious.
2. Provide order, beauty, and the gracious extras of life.
3. Ask about their favorite art; and encourage them to express themselves freely in that area.

How do you behave around someone who is not esthetic? Relax and turn your attention to other traits that jump out at you.

*   *   *   *   *

A flare for the dramatic

DRAMATIC

The high, sweeping, arched eyebrow is the indicator of a flare for the dramatic. So many actresses have this type of eyebrow that many girls and women pluck their eyebrows in order to look more like the actresses they admire.

The dramatic person has a gift for mimicking and feels the spirit of the situation. They can fit into any role. Lucille Ball is a good prototype; as is Fred Astaire, who added so much style to his dancing.

Feeling the story line, the dramatic person makes effective entrances and sweeping exits. A flower in the hair adds a theatrical touch, as well as costumes, jewelry, make-up, hairstyles and hats. The parade marshal, the drum major and the majorette are all more effective if they possess this flare for the dramatic.

What to do around someone dramatic:

1. Get them to help bring your party to life.
2. Bear in mind that their dramatic behavior is not false or put on, but that they are really that way, and enjoy it. Let them help you create displays.
3. Take them to plays or present them with videos.

If the dramatic trait is absent, these suggestions are not applicable, but there will be other traits to notice.

HUMOR

You can tease people who have laugh lines fanning out from the outside corner of their eyes. But, if you try to tease someone who has no such lines, your joke is liable to go over "like a lead balloon."

If you've been on this planet very long, you have seen occasions where humor was invaluable. It takes the edge off tension. I have seen the tide turned at a legislative hearing by a witness injecting humor.

What a lubricant humor is! Good humor is infectious. The human spirit enjoys being released constructively. That is why programs like Bill Cosby's get number one ratings.

Humor

If you lack humor yourself, you can develop it (and add to you skill and popularity) by: 1) entering situations good-humoredly, as if you were going to a picnic; 2) using common courtesies, such as "Thank you," "How nice of you!" and "What a nice day!" and 3) talking about things that are pleasant. These are the stages that make you ready to do the Bob Hope bit if you want.

What should you do around others with humor or the lack of it?

If you're around someone with a good sense of humor:

1. You can be more at ease and less defensive.
2. Enjoy their company and invite them to your parties.
3. If you are hiring, remember a good sense of humor is a must for a good salesman, waitress or nurse.

But, if you are with someone who lacks a sense of humor:

1. Don't try to kid.
2. Take them as they are. They have other virtues.
3. Have someone else around as a counter-balance.

Rhetoric

RHETORIC

Those little lines fanning out from the inner corner of the eye and traveling beneath the eye toward the cheekbone indicate rhetoric — a feeling for the precise word or for the flow of words. Babies don't have them. Small children seldom have them. Some adults don't possess them. This is a trait that has to be developed.

If you are a woman, be proud of these lines. No use trying to get rid of them or rub them out with cold cream. They won't go away, unless you stop paying attention to exact words and vocabulary over an extended period of time.

These lines are numerous and pronounced on someone with a real gift for the exact word, such as Walter Cronkite.

To the possessor of this trait, there is quite a difference in meaning between two words such as "popular" and "fashionable." He or she may even enjoy reading the dictionary.

To this person, the word that just fits is like making a hole-in-one in golf. The wrong word, or a misspelled or mispronounced word, is irritating.

What to do around someone with pronounced rhetoric:

1. Enjoy their skillful use of precise words, and learn as many new words from them as possible.
2. Ask them about words of which you are uncertain.
3. Do not challenge their pronunciation or spelling.

What to do around those with little rhetoric:

1. Expect one-syllable words.
2. Don't waste fancy words of your own.
3. Expect more general and less descriptive language.

*   *   *   *   *

Judgment variation

JUDGMENT

Each eye feeds images to both sides of the brain where binocular fusion takes place. When the eyes sit on the same level, the two pictures fed back into the brain are more similar.

With some people, including perhaps yourself, one eye sits higher than the other. Where this is noticeably the case, it has been determined in structure/function research that the individual tends to have unusual judgment, and is able to come up with a unique slant on the subject. Christopher Columbus is a good example. He said that the world was round when all the authorities of 1491 agreed that it was flat.

This quality of variations in judgment from the usual is an example that no human quality is good or bad by itself, but only as it is used. It can be a great asset in inventing, such as the first jet plane or transistor. It is a gift in creative fields, such as the dream sequence that Katherine DeMille put in the stage production of "Oklahoma." But, the famous painter Whistler, early in his career, got fired from his job as a Navy cartographer because he drew mermaids on the maps.

If you have a case coming up before a judge, you hope he is completely level-eyed and conventional and will not take off on some unusual tack.

If you are dealing with someone who has high judgment variation:

1. Get them in on creative discussions or jobs.
2. Expect unusual slants in ideas or behavior.
3. Make rules and regulations plain to them.

If you are around someone built more conventionally:

1. Keep quiet about your far out ideas.
2. Expect predictable behavior that follows standard lines.
3. Check with them if you want to find out the rules and regulations and how something is customarily done.

Exacting

Exacting — getting too fussy

Exactingness, high

EXACTING

You were not born with those worry lines, and you can get rid of them if you want to badly enough.

The other day, my wife and I were at a wedding reception and a woman came up to us and said, "I did what you told me three years ago and I got rid of my worry lines."

"Exactly what did I tell you?" I asked.

"To handle things just once," was her reply.

It's that simple. Those worry lines between the eyebrows come from worrying. No more double-checking. When you are locking the car, hold the key consciously in one hand while you close the door with the other. Then, overcome that tendency later to look in your purse or feel in your pocket to see if you brought the key.

If you notice worry lines up and down between someone's eyebrows, you know that, although that individual has a noble soul inside, he or she is going to be a fussbudget — wanting every little thing just so, doubting themselves and going back over matters a second time.

What to do around someone who is exacting:

1. Be glad it's them instead of you. You have better digestion and are more carefree.
2. Have every little thing exactly the way he or she wants. If it's three-minute eggs, don't cook them two minutes and 45 seconds. If he wants one-inch margins in typing, give them to him — it is a cheap way to keep him happy!
3. Remind them that you have followed their idea. This will make a hit (but don't expect them to tell you so).

If you are around someone free of worry lines:

1. You can be more at ease.
2. Expect the person to be more companionable.
3. Remember, you will still have to watch other traits.

*   *   *   *   *

Observant of detail

DETAIL CONCERN

In his autobiography, Benjamin Franklin admitted that the trait that caused him the most trouble was detail concern. Big things he could take in stride, but a troublesome detail, such as misplacing something, would spoil his day.

The physical indicator for detail concern is a pair of small bony protuberances in the lower part of the forehead, just over the inner part of the eyebrows. These bony developments under the skin and on each side of the worry lines may be as small as a lima bean or much larger.

No one is born with these indicators and their size depends upon how much of a detail-oriented person the individual has become.

Details are important, as tragically demonstrated by the space shuttle explosion moments after take off. But, the trick is to take care of the details properly as part of the big picture, and not let little things upset you or "get your goat." (As Pat replied when Mike came along and observed that Pat was laying bricks, "Oh no, we're building a cathedral!")

What to do around someone who has developed detail concern:

1. Take care of the little details that involve them. It's a cheap way to keep them happy. If they want a button sewed, sew it right away. Then, put a little note in the pocket, "I'm so glad I've got you to sew it for."

2. Avoid sharing any troublesome detail you have encountered, or they will be bothered and lecture you on how to avoid that in the future. If a faucet leaks, don't bother them, call a plumber and pay for it out of your own funds.

3. Be glad it's them instead of you — you are able to take small things better in stride.

What about dealing with someone who has an unclouded, smooth brow with no sign of detail concern? This trait is not applicable then. But there will be other traits that will jump out at you.

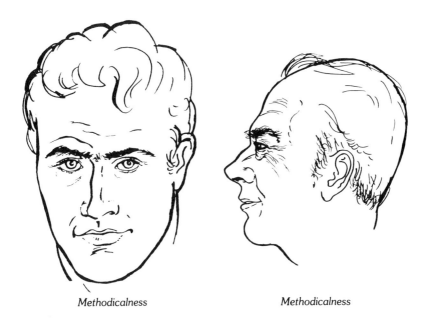

Methodicalness   *Methodicalness*

METHODICALNESS

When I did research at San Quentin prison, it was easy to tell how long different men had been in there — those who had been in the "big house" the longest got the highest scores on methodicalness. For years, these men had been doing the same thing, at the same hour, eating the same kind of food on certain days out of the same partitioned area of the plate.

Technically, methodicalness is indicated by "hyper-plasia of the supra-orbital margin." In everyday language, there is a ledge in the lower part of the forehead. This bony protuberance is just above the eyebrows. In extreme cases, this ledge may extend clear across the lower part of the forehead.

Speaking personologically, this is a "how" trait instead of a "what" trait. The methodical person is used to doing a certain thing a certain way and with certain equipment, and heaven help you if you upset this routine. The wife of a highly methodical man knows when he is going to engage in sex before he realizes it (usually on Saturday night so he can sleep late on Sunday). She has learned his little signs.

More often, it is men rather than women who become highly methodical. But, women can be that way too.

What to do when you notice someone is decidedly methodical:

1. Tell the methodical person 14 days ahead of time what you would like done, so he can work it into his own system.
2. Keep his socks matched and where he expects to find them. Make the kids put his tools back where they found them.
3. Give them extra credit if they don't frown or protest when you want to change arrangements at the last minute. This is real graciousness on their part.

These suggestions are not applicable when you are around someone lacking this trait.

Three
Mouth-Area Traits

GENEROSITY AND CONCISENESS

Generous   *Concise — doesn't waste words,*   *Automatic giving*
time or materials

Roughly speaking, generous lips indicate a generous disposition. But, only roughly speaking, because there are other traits, such as stubbornness and acquisitiveness, that can prevent a person from pouring out all he or she has.

Nevertheless, full lips are so often associated with an outpouring nature, that women with tight, thin lips often fudge with their lipstick to make their lips more appealing.

Like any other trait, being a giver is not good or bad except as directed. Being generous with one's time and efforts is fine in nursing, homemaking, social work, etc. As a credit manager or loan officer, it can be a handicap unless it's controlled. Recent photographic research concluded that the most successful bankers have small, tight lips, and eyes that are close together.

You will notice that those with concise lips tend to act concisely. They talk like Western Union. They get to the point right away. They do not waste gestures, time or material. They get misunderstood as being curt or in a hurry by large-lipped people who are not used to talking so quickly themselves.

What to do around those inclined to be generous:

1. Expect the conversation or action to take longer.
2. Know you are more liable to get what you ask for.
3. Feel more free to ask for help or favors.

What to do when you're with a tight-lipped, concise person:

1. Don't irritate them by being verbose.
2. Do not be hurt by their shortness or silence.
3. Anticipate brevity and efficiency.

*   *   *   *   *

Optimistic   *Pessimistic, mouth corners down*

OPTIMISM AND PESSIMISM

Optimism and pessimism. These traits are so old that they were recognized and used in the masks of the actors of ancient Greece. The happy, upturned mouth symbolized comedy, and the sad, drooping mouth symbolized tragedy.

Our mouth betrays us. If our thoughts are generally gloomy, we develop a "sourpuss." It is indeed as Abraham Lincoln once said, "The dear Lord gave us our face, but we make our own mouth."

People sense how the mouth indicates disposition. To look more attractive, we smile when we are being photographed. On a visit to the Kodak factory in Rochester, N.Y., the tour hostess told us as we were being photographed, "Look like you have just been given a raise."

We are informed that anatomically it takes fewer muscles to smile than to frown. But, human nature is such that all too often it is easier to be negative and pessimistic than positive and optimistic. We cannot build on the negative; we can only build on the positive.

So, for many reasons it pays to accentuate the positive. Here are some proven tips along that line. Follow the Optimist Club creed: "Think only of the best, work only for the best, and expect only the best. Wear a cheerful countenance at all times, and greet every living creature you meet with a smile."

What to do if you are around a pessimist:

1. Expect pessimism, so don't share your dreams or you will get cold water poured on them.
2. Talk "positive" (constructively) to keep up your own morale. Whistle, hum or sing something light, such as "Yankee Doodle" or "Deep in the Heart of Texas."
3. Get out as soon as you can, and find an optimist to be around.

What to do if you are around an optimist:

1. Celebrate. Here's somebody all too rare and who's fun to be with.
2. You can share your news or knowledge without having a "wet blanket" thrown at them.
3. Invite them to your parties and in hiring, give them extra consideration or favor.

Impetuous — speaks before thinking   *Not impetuous — thinks before speaking*

Impetuosity High (left) Low (right)

IMPETUOUSNESS

Seen from the side, the impetuous person's mouth protrudes out in front more than it does on most people.

Like any other human trait, this trait is only good or bad according to how it is directed. Properly directed, it provides the gifts of speaking and swift movement (which is especially important in a sport like basketball).

In contrast, the individual with relatively little mouth or lips protruding from that part of the face is more deliberate.

What to do around someone impetuous:

1. Expect more talking.
2. Expect swift action, especially in traffic.
3. Caution them around dangerous equipment.

What to do around someone who is more deliberate:

1. Don't misinterpret their less conversational nature as meaning they are not interested or that they are unhappy with you.
2. Expect to have to draw them out more in conversation.
3. Value their judgment.

ORAL EXPRESSION

Women particularly are interested in face lines.

Not all lines are "bad." In fact, most of them indicate favorable aspects of personality. (Speaking personologically, the only face lines indicating something undesirable are the worry lines that run up and down between the eyebrows — the tell-tale mark of fussiness and exactingness.)

If you have lines running from the outer edge of the nostrils to the outer edge of your mouth, these lines indicate a knack at oral expression — you can say things like you mean them, and people remember what you say. They may quote you a week later.

You will notice these lines frequently on lawyers, actors, lecturers, teachers — people who say things with unction, good timing or deep feeling.

Oral expression

Look in the mirror and say something as if you really mean it. You will see the creases for these lines appear.

What to do around someone with high oral expression:

1. Expect this person to more likely mean what he or she says.
2. Expect him or her to be more persuasive.
3. Have him or her persuade others for you.

What to do around others lacking this characteristic:

1. Expect less deliberate expression.
2. Give them extra credit if they do express deeply.
3. Remember that they can develop this quality if they want to.

Pride in personal appearance

PRIDE IN
PERSONAL APPEARANCE

Some people have a knack for knowing how to look good, and for helping other people to look their best. Brooke Shields is a prototype.

If you look at any fashion model or beautician, you will notice that they have an unusually short distance between their nose and mouth. This is the physical indicator for pride in personal appearance — how a person looks visually. Take somebody built this way along with you for guidance when you are choosing apparel, jewelry, cosmetics or hairstyle.

When you are dealing with someone built this way:

1. Value their advice on matters of personal appearance.
2. Expect them to take longer to dress and get ready.

3. Know that if you give them clothing as a gift, they won't wear it unless it does more for them than what they already have.

Special note: The opposite build from pride in appearance indicates a complete difference in the kind of trait — just as brown eyes are different from blue eyes. It is a difference in kind rather than a difference in degree. An unusually large space between nose and mouth is the indicator for a quality called **dry wit.**

Dry wit

DRY WIT

A prototype for dry wit is the nonegenarian entertainer George Burns. You may recall his quip when jibed about going out with women so much younger rather than women his own age: "There ARE no women my age."

The possessor of dry wit has a way of summing up the essence in a humorous way — saying things with humorous reaction that other people could not get away with saying.

In dealing with someone with dry wit:

1. Expect curt summaries.
2. Enlist them to speak to groups.
3. Remember that they won't be much interested in compliments about personal appearance. Compliment them instead about achievements.

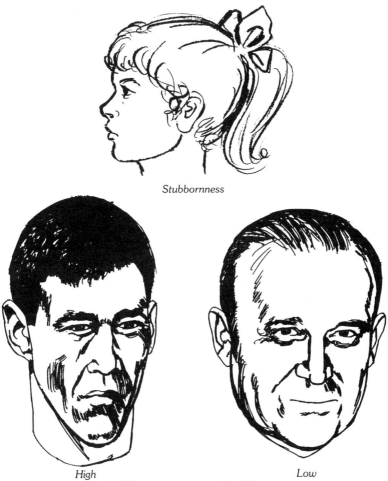

Stubbornness

High   *Low*

Stubbornness — automatic resistance

STUBBORNNESS

Automatic resistance is indicated by the V-shaped chin (the more bird-like shape of the lower part of the face).

This trait is perhaps the best illustration that no human quality is good or bad except as it is directed. Properly used, it indicates strength of character; such as preventing someone from getting "hooked" on narcotics. Improperly used, it is mulishness and has spoiled many marriages, especially the sexual aspect of the relationship.

So, what do you do when you are around the stubborn person with the V-shaped chin?

1. Remember "please" is the magic word — or, "If it meets with your approval."
2. Don't raise your voice or sound bossy, or you will create unnecessary resistance.
3. Expect NO the first time you bring something up.

On the other hand, if you're around someone with more of a flat chin area:

1. Expect more compliance, you are dealing with a more tractable person.
2. Anticipate that this is someone who is easier to deal with.
3. You can be more relaxed. You need not be so careful about your tone of voice or how you speak.

PUGNACITY

The disposition to be pugnacious is indicated by the "bulldog chin" — a relatively broad, flat chin.

It is hard to think of any boxer with a weak chin. The word "pugnacity" and the word "pugilist," come from the same Latin root, "pugnus," meaning fist.

It depends on other traits whether the pugnacious individual will start the fight, but he will finish it. Winston Churchill was a good example of this, both visually and literally, as he said "Sink the Bismarck!"

Pugnacity

The pugnacious individual actually welcomes a good scrap, once he or she gets into it. The human race is fortunate to have wholesome outlets for this trait, such as boxing, martial arts and other contact sports, so that people with this trait can express it without starting a war.

If you are pugnacious:

1. Know how to defend yourself in case you do get involved in a dispute.
2. Participate in contact sports.
3. Don't start the fight yourself.

When you're around someone who has this trait:

1. Avoid challenging them, especially physically.
2. Remember that they enjoy a fight.
3. If you have the opportunity, guide them into contact sports.

If someone scores low on this trait, these suggestions are not applicable.

Four
Facial Traits

INNATE SELF-CONFIDENCE

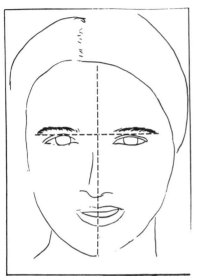
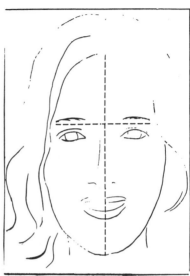

High self-confidence (left)
Low self-confidence (right)

Self-confident —
no clinging vine

Low self-confidence —
sells self short

Low self-confidence —
easily discouraged

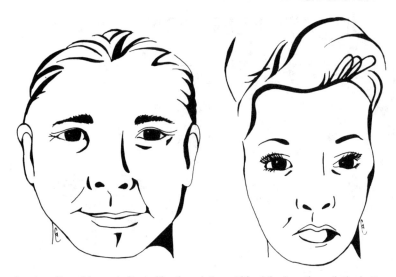

Innate self confidence, indicated by the relative width of the face through the bottom part of the forehead

Think of the people you know. Those with a broad face have natural confidence and are inclined to take charge. In a marriage or business partnership, it is the person with this trait who usually ends up making the basic decisions. It is not that this individual is more capable or intelligent, he or she just FEELS that they are.

To make a comparison, it is much like the bulldog and the collie. The collie is more beautiful and intelligent, but when the bulldog moves into the scene, there is no question about who is in charge.

The exact indicator for this trait is the relative width of a person's forehead through the eyebrows in comparison to the height of the face. It is not inches or pounds, it is a relative proportion. Again, it is not the size of the dog in the fight, it is the size of the fight in the dog.

In research studies involving World War II combat soldiers who had been wounded, it was found that the physical location for the ego was in the prefrontal lobes of the brain. When they were shot or injured there, their ego was also damaged. Ward Halstead reported this in his 1952 book, "Brain and Intelligence."

However, in today's society, the word "ego" is clouded too much with a negative connotation of "egotistical." Therefore, in biological personality, the term "innate self-confidence" is used.

The great thing about human nature is that we can consciously direct our constitutional qualities, just as we can direct the movement of our arms. Not only can a quality like innate self-confidence be directed, it can be amplified or changed over a period of time. The person with a narrow face who, by nature, underrates himself or herself and is too self-conscious, can learn to build confidence — and, even to enjoy speaking up or taking over. Many a person has learned to be less self-conscious, and to take over and lead by joining a speaker's club, such as Toastmasters.

Wives with this trait can learn not to wear the pants but rather to use their strength to build up their less-confident husbands. They can also learn to freely use their leadership on their own projects.

Winston Churchill was a great example of the broad-faced man who used his indomitable self-confidence and courage to inspire an entire nation during war-time crisis.

What to do around someone high in self-confidence:

1. Talk in big terms. Say, for example, "While we're at it, how about putting in a swimming pool?"
2. Be thorough. Have your homework done. Contempt will be shown for weakness and irritation demonstrated at inadequacy.
3. Don't start anything you're not going to finish. This goes for children as well, even as young as two years. With discipline, either do it or don't do it. Do not just talk about it, or the broad-faced one will blandly ignore you and do whatever he or she pleases.

What to do around someone innately low in self-confidence:

1. Pay them a compliment. Tell them something you have noticed that they did well, or comment on something you appreciate about them.

2. Remember, they only feel comfortable going forward one step at a time. Do not throw the whole thing at them at once.

3. Remember, they need frequent encouragement until they outgrow their inner feeling of inadequacy. When they have demonstrated to themselves a few times that they can do something, they will move in on it just as confidently as anyone else. Meanwhile, tell them, "I know you can do it."

*   *   *   *   *

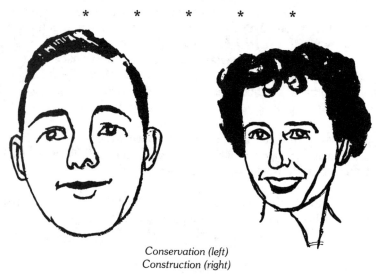

Conservation (left)
Construction (right)

CONSERVATION AND CONSTRUCTION

As Dr. William Sheldon points out in his classic book, "The Varieties of Human Physique," there are, in general, three basic groups of human structure: endomorph, mesomorph and ectomorph.

The roundish endomorphs have a large proportion of endoderm (digestive tissue) compared to other people. They are great on food, entertainment, and human comfort. They are born cooks, hosts and politicians. They are jovial and gregarious. They settle down and make the most of everything, including lovemaking. They hate to see anything go to waste. They are conservative. They combine errands and are strong on conservation in any form.

The mesomorph, who has a more muscular square build, has a relatively high proportion of mesoderm, the middle of the three primary germ layers of the embryo that develop into the skeletal and muscular systems. These are the people who build, dig, and change the face of the earth. They are career-minded, more than homemakers. They are project people who get wrapped up in their work. Women as well as men can be this way, and, as much as these people love their family, they feel as if their feet were set in cement if they find themselves trapped in a routine.

The ectomorphs, those with a triangular-shaped face and large crown on the top of the head, like Sir Bertram Russell the famous philosopher, are rare. They have a comparatively high proportion of ectoderm (nervous tissue). They are the thinkers. They respond more mentally than physically. That is what to expect when you find one.

Now, let us turn our attention to the more numerous round-faced, conservative individuals, and the squarely built, constructive individuals.

If you are around a conservative person:

1. Ask them about their home.
2. Try to get invited to dinner; also ask them about the best restaurants and places to buy food.
3. Please them by seeing that no food is allowed to spoil, and that nothing that could possibly be used is thrown out.

If you are around a constructive person:

1. Remember that his or her career comes first — expect little time to be devoted to home.

2. Anticipate little attention to rest or food; this person eats to live rather than living to eat.

3. Get animation into the conversation by asking about career achievements, plans and activities.

PHYSICAL INSULATION

Physical insulation
High (left)
Low (right)

Low physical insulation —
dainty texture

Low physical insulation

Hair, skin and nervous tissue are linked genetically. When a new human being is conceived, even before the basic cell has divided into 16, one of the cells becomes the one that produces these three components of our structure.

Hair is the easiest component of this structural package to measure.

Some people you know have "baby hair" and a silken fiber. If you stop to think, you will realize that they are more sensitive, both physically and emotionally. Indeed, they act more "thin-skinned." And, they have a finer mannerism, more subtlety and finesse, to go with their more delicate texture. Other traits being equal, men built this way have a more gentle demeanor — the late great actor Sir Alec Guiness is a good example.

Individuals built with coarser hair and more rugged fiber, have more of a robust and hearty way of functioning. They can withstand more physically, are less dainty, and are survivors. They can dish it out as well as take it. They need more than a gentle hint to be impressed. Clark Gable had this build, and is still remembered for his swashbuckling and masterful role in "Gone With The Wind."

I have run statistics on hair measurements of hundreds of people, and most often, it is the woman who is more thin-skinned and dainty. But, not always. There are plenty of women who have a "Tugboat Annie" streak in them. And, there are plenty of men who are on the refined, gentle side.

It is true that, more often than not, the husband is usually built coarser and cruder and can unintentionally offend his more dainty mate. This brings about the situation exemplified in the French saying, "There are no frigid wives, just clumsy husbands."

The genetic components of hair, skin and nervous tissue affect not only our physical tastes, such as in food or temperature, but also our dispositions. The more ruggedly built person is more of a survivor, but in a personal situation, it may take them longer to "get the message."

Always, it is the extremes that create the individuality.

There are plenty of people built in the middle range on this trait. They can accommodate reasonably well to a coarse situation or to a cultured and refined environment. It is with individuals who have either the "silken" or the "burlap" fiber to whom you must make the most adjustment if you are built differently.

What to do around someone with rugged fiber and texture:

1. Talk louder and make bigger gestures to make sure your message is received.
2. Expect them to like more heavily seasoned foods and in larger amounts; also clothing with coarser weave and more vibrant colors.
3. Accommodate their love of the outdoors and vigorous action.

What to do around someone with a dainty build:

1. Use finesse, show subtlety, and exhibit culture and refinement.
2. Expect expensive tastes and the need for quality instead of

quantity; take them to the "Regency" rather than the cheap diner.

3. Give them extra credit if they rough it with you. Remember, they are really suffering if they have to go too long without hot and cold running water and a private bath.

HARD, SOFT OR ELASTIC

Current body tone
Hard (left)
Soft (right)

Here, we are dealing with a trait that can be changed fairly rapidly.

Some people have allowed themselves to become soft in their body tone. Their flesh is jelly-like. Their dispositions are impression-able and liable to be wishy-washy. Their voice is inclined to drag or whine. They have little energy or follow-through. They are overly responsive to obstacles and to their own thoughts. But, they can toughen up when they decide to and regain their old bounce and resiliency. They can become firmer in certain situations.

In contrast, think of anyone you know whose flesh is hard and tough — THEY are hard and tough. You cannot easily make a dent in them (literally or figuratively). They are genuine and firm. When they do decide to respond, the respond sincerely and then carry through.

In between these two extremes, are the elastic and bouncy people. These are the ones with enthusiasm and resiliency. They have vim, vigor, verve and vitality. They are full of life and most likely fun to be around. They fit more easily into situations — they can bend more with the breeze, so to speak. This quality is everyone's natural heritage. We were all born with it. If we have lost it, we should work actively to build it back up.

What to do around someone who is hard:

1. Remember, they are not going to respond too quickly or easily, but they will respond wholeheartedly when they do. Keep at it.
2. Remember, that since they have become wooden, they only SEEM to not understand your point of view. Don't let the poker face mislead you.
3. Count on them for sincerity.

What to do around someone who is soft:

1. Expect whining. Watch out — they are good at exercising the "tyranny of weakness" and getting you to do things for them. Don't let them work you.
2. Remember, they are liable to back out later without telling you. Get a signature and a deposit, and check on them later.
3. Remember, they can toughen up, if and when they want to.

If you are around someone who is elastic and flexible, enjoy this side of their nature, and their pleasant company.

Reacts physically   *Reacts mentally*

PHYSICAL OR MENTAL MOTIVE

People with a lot of physical energy usually have, proportionately, a large amount of face under the nose. Usually, they have either been in athletics or are interested in them. A prototype is Muhamed Ali, the former heavyweight boxing champion.

The opposite is the individual with a relatively small amount of face below the nose. Occasionally, they even have a V-shaped face. A prototype is the late philosopher Sir Bertram Russell, who was high on mental energy rather than physical energy or endurance.

When with the individual with relatively strong physical motive:

1. Expect physical activity and physical restlessness.
2. Provide them with things to do and places to go.
3. Anticipate them setting quite a pace for anyone to follow.

When with someone with relatively low physical motive:

1. Expect their reaction to be more mental.
2. Provide mental activities, such as discussion, reading and chess.
3. Anticipate less interest in being on the go just for the sake of being on the go.

*   *   *   *   *

Adventurousness

ADVENTUROUSNESS

What do the faces of the American Indians, Mongols and Vikings have visually in common? They all have high, prominent cheek bones. Their common factors in functioning are travel, movement and adventurousness.

If you want to strike up conversation with someone who has high or prominent cheek bones, ask "Where have you traveled?" or "If you could travel, where would you like to go?"

The adventurous person likes variety, change, excitement, unfoldment, trying new things, and doing old things in new ways. These are the spice of life to the adventurous, whether in lovemaking or at work.

Surprises. Unfoldment. A gift to your loved one isn't really a gift unless it's giftwrapped.

Of course, the biggest adventure in life is your own self-unfoldment, but that's the subject for another book. If you're interested now, expand your capacities by working each week on best expressing one of your own traits.

What to do around the adventurous individual:

1. Draw them out about their travel hopes, plans and experiences.
2. Plan surprise events for them. Present surprise gifts, giftwrapped of course.
3. Be more lively and innovative around them. Avoid monotony. Take them places, especially new or different places.

If an individual scores low on this trait, these suggestions are not applicable.

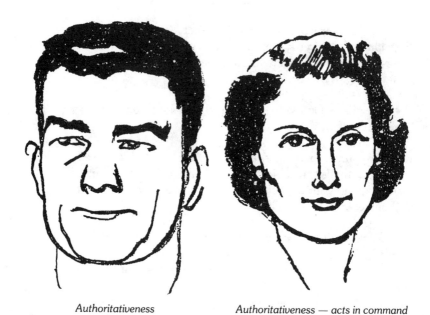

Authoritativeness   *Authoritativeness — acts in command*

AUTHORITATIVENESS

If you call to mind those you know, both male and female, who have a broad "admiral's jaw," you will find that they all have a commanding nature. Whether or not they take charge, you feel that they could. And, you pay attention to their pronouncements: it sounds like the oracle. They sound convincing.

They never back down. Winston Churchill is the prototype: "We will fight them from the fields. . .we will NEVER surrender."

Other traits being equal, those with a broad jaw have more physical courage. They can handle large animals. (This trait may make the difference in whether a child can handle a pony or horse.)

Some points on what to do around someone authoritative:

1. Don't try to force them to back down. If they are getting into

the parking space first, give it to them.
    2. Don't expect to hear "please" and "thank you."
    3. Get them on your team, in a commanding position if possible.

Some points on what to do around someone lacking
authoritativeness:

    1. Do not expect physical courage.
    2. Anticipate others to pay less attention to what they say.
    3. If you are giving a pet, make it a small animal or a bird.

Self-reliance
High (left)
Low (right)

INSTINCTIVE SELF-RELIANCE

Most aviators usually have a noticeable flair to their nostrils.
They possess a trait called instinctive self-reliance. They are not
tentative. They are decisive. They have a distinct feeling of just when
to zoom up off the ground and just when to lower the flaps to land.

Surgeons are the same way in style of procedure. Likewise with basketball stars — no uncertainty, no indefiniteness.

Instinctive self-reliance has to do with style of procedure. Whether the individual has the courage to launch the procedure requires another trait.

Some people are courageous enough for the project, but lack the confidence of knowing that their way would work best. They are like the man who was brave enough to grab the bull by the horn, but didn't know which horn. Such an individual has less leadership ability and listens to too many people's advice. You know people who are this way, who always need someone to go along with them to hold their hand, so to speak. They are the ones who lack a flare of the nostrils. They should have few advisors, make up their own minds, and call their soul their own.

Being self-reliant doesn't mean that the individual knows the best way to do it — he or she just FEELS that their way would work best. If they lack traits, such as good judgment, their idea may not be worth much. Much like the man whose little nephew asked, "Uncle, if you're so smart, why aren't you rich?"

Being a born advisor, the self-reliant person can make himself or herself unpopular when giving unsolicited advice — such as the mother-in-law telling the young wife how to stuff the turkey or how to take care of the baby.

What to do around the highly self-reliant:

1. Let them do it their way, if you can. They probably will do it anyway, even if it means going broke!
2. Expect little delegation of authority by them (they will try to do it all themselves and pick the chickens too.)
3. Ask for their advice — they love to give it.

Things to remember when dealing with a person low on instinctive self-reliance:

1. You can freely advise them.
2. Be supportive.
3. Expect them to go to other people for advice after they have already asked you.

* * * * *

Acquisitiveness — likes to accumulate   *Acquisitiveness, high*

ACQUISITIVENESS

Open your wallet, take out a one dollar bill and look at the picture of George Washington, the country's first millionaire. Notice how the head steadily gets wider as it goes back from the mouth to the ears. (The head is widest between the ears.)

This is the physical indicator for acquisitiveness. People with this trait have good management skills, are providential and acquiring, take good care of belongings, and live within their means. Some, jokingly call this trait "scotch."

The acquisitive person works industriously to get ahead. If he's stationed in the military service and has opportunity to work weekends, he will take on some job, such a service station attendant to bring in additional money. He works to own instead of renting, and to earn interest rather than paying. He will study harder to gain rank or a position of more advantage.

Their body is one of their possessions, so they are inclined to take better care of it and thus, will live longer. Seldom does an acquisitive person allow himself or herself to become an alcoholic. They have worked very hard for what they have, and are going to hang on to it. They are great on security.

The contrasting build, the person with low acquisitive tendencies, is such that the head narrows back toward the ears (the head is narrowest between the ears). Here is the happy-go-lucky person who lives from day to day — and, all to often, from hand to mouth.

If your contact is with an acquisitive individual:

1. Ask their advice on long-range financial matters, such as property, as well as on short-range matters; for instance, where you can buy something wholesale.
2. Know they have plenty of assets in spite of their "crying towel." Talk about taxes, high prices and lazy, inadequate help.
3. Remember they have other traits and aspects to their nature. Such as, if they are generous, they will give you a ride, but they will not cosign a note for you unless you have collateral!

If you are dealing with an unacquisitive person:

1. Enjoy their ability to live for today without worrying about tomorrow, and their carefree, unselfish attitude.
2. Be careful about getting involved in their finances — they are going to have to develop their own thriftiness. Suggest that they wait until they have saved up enough to pay cash for it.
3. Expect them to be willing to buy now and pay later, but verify their credit.

Special note: If there is a mood swing on this trait, then when the individual is in the thrifty mood, they will work hard to get something; but, in the other mood, like Robin Hood, they will give it away and not take care of it.

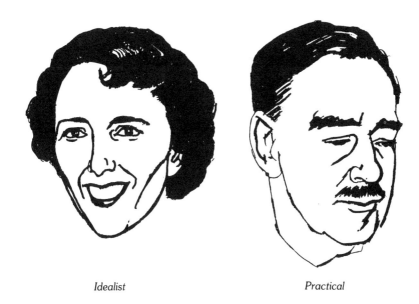

Idealist   *Practical*

IDEALIZING

The indication for the idealist is that there is a relatively large amount of brain above the ear compared to most people. The ear may sit so low that the ear opening is as low as the nose opening. Another way of looking at it is that the ear sits close to the collar. It is best seen in profile.

The less idealistic, more practical person is built with the ear higher on the head. This person is more down-to-earth, more practical, less of a romanticist, less wrapped up in a principle or a cause, less upset by what he finds in life, and more willing to take what "goes with the territory."

As with all traits, remember that if the score is in the middle range, the behavior will be in the middle range and therefore worth little attention. It is always the extremes that count; the "peaks and valleys" of personality.

The sheer idealist is "stuffed with stardust." Here is the person who longs for the noble or lofty and who will devote years to, or even die for a principle or cause.

The idealist feels a need to help mankind move more toward the ideal, and often gravitates into one of the professions. This is the hero-worshiper. He or she sees the possibilities in people and puts them up on a pedestal (then, is disenchanted or disillusioned when they turn out to be human).

If you are dealing with an idealist:

1. Remember that they have you up on a pedestal. If you hit your thumb with a hammer, don't say that naughty word! Be on your best behavior.
2. If it's a woman, send flowers.
3. Draw her or him out about their lofty hops and goals.

If you're dealing with someone less idealistic:

1. Talk about everyday matters.
2. Expect them to be ready to get going and not wait for the perfect time, place, equipment, or person.
3. Get them to predict for you how certain individuals are going to behave.

Sympathetic

SYMPATHY

If it's sympathy you're looking for, go to someone who has big "goo-goo" eyes and large red lips — that's the one to whom you can pour your heart out, and who will feel for you. If you go instead to someone with little beady eyes and a mouth like a bear trap, you are liable to hear, "Well, what did you expect?" instead of, "Oh, too bad!"

The large eyes denote affectionateness and outward emotionality. The full, large lips are linked with generosity and automatic giving.

What to do if you are with a sympathetic person:

1. Expect free demonstration of pity.
2. Go to that person for compassion if you need it.

3. Remember they are liable to feel sorry for themselves and indulge in self-pity, so bear with them reasonably in this regard.

What to do if you are with an unsympathetic person:

1. Anticipate matter-of-fact handling of situations.
2. Remember that underneath they do have sympathy, but, with their build, their tendency is to save it for real emergencies.
3. If you're in personnel, put them into positions like bill collecting, where controlled compassion is an asset.

* * * * *

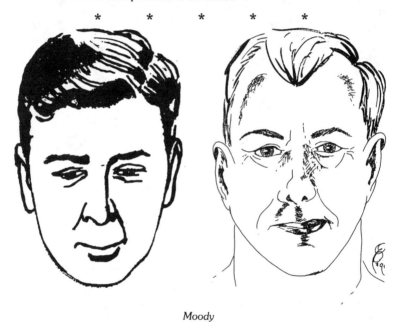

Moody

MOODS

The degree of difference between one side of the face and the other, is the key to how much the individual changes with their mood. And, just how different some people can be, according to the mood they're in, is surprising!

Just as our fingerprints are different in our two hands, so we are different in the two sides of our face. We have two profiles. President Lyndon Johnson had the press gallery sit on a particular side because they would then photograph his face from the side he thought looked best.

The reason one side is different from the other is genetic. We get 23 chromosomes from each parent. With meiosis and mitosis, our maternal and paternal contributions blend, but we still have bilateral asymmetry. In a manner of speaking, one side of us more represents our mother's heritage, and the other side our father's. I have a son who has one ear noticeably like mine and the other like his mother's.

Galen, the ancient Greek physician, thought that males were conceived from the right ovary because usually, but not always, that side of the face is more representative of the paternal heritage.

Due to the crossover of nerves from brain to body, one side of the brain governs the opposite side of the body. Usually the right (creative) brain hemisphere, which goes with the left side of the body, corresponds to the heritage from the feminine parent.

Now, let's turn from HOW we got to be different on on side to WHAT to do about it in dealing with others.

We all have moods, but in different degrees. Very seldom will you find a true Jekyll and Hyde. But, with those whose two profiles are noticeably different, you can expect drastic mood swings.

And, it's not difficult to tell which mood someone is in. The eyes, the tone of voice, the posture and the attitude all tell you at once. Behave accordingly.

When with the person who has pronounced moods:

1. Cash in on the high moods. Offer your ideas, requests or proposals then. Enjoy their good spirit.
2. If the other person is in a low mood, hold your bright idea for

later. Be nice and on the quiet side. Do things you know the other
person likes, or offer a favorite food or beverage. Do not be
surprised if it is turned down. Remember, the mood will pass.

3. If the other person in in a low mood, remember that it's just
their natural rhythm or something they have done. Don't flatter
yourself that you caused it and don't call attention to their bad
mood. Be friendly and courteous. Unless the other wants to talk or
unload, get back to your own affairs as soon as you can.

When with the person who has few moods:

1. Enjoy their even disposition.
2. Expect no brilliance or slumps.
3. Know you can anticipate how they will be feeling.

*   *   *   *   *

High comprehension — intellectual   *High comprehension*

COMPREHENSION

The general ability to comprehend all facets of a situation is
indicated physically by a relatively high, broad forehead that is also

rather full and high, as viewed from the side. All of this is in proportion to the head as a whole. (And, of course, as with all traits, this in not measured in inches or pounds, but the comparative proportion within the individual.)

This is the individual who sees the potential in a situation, is resourceful and generally on the intellectual side.

The person with a great deal of comprehension can see a lot of possibilities, but is not necessarily clever or smart in little everyday affairs. Someone once said, "nothing is as uncommon as common sense." That ability depends on judgment factors and other traits.

What to do around those with a deep ability to comprehend:

1. Enjoy their grasp of subjects and possibilities.
2. Expect them to complicate matters.
3. Get them to simplify where possible and to do the obvious.

What to do around those not overloaded with this quality:

1. Remember, they are very good in some specialized area rather than knowing everything about everybody and everything.
2. Expect less complication.
3. Anticipate practicality (beer and the Dodgers).

Leadership

LEADERSHIP

If you think of the leaders you know, you will see that they all lead in different manners. Some are buoyant and inspiring. Others, win by covering all their bases and not alienating good people.

But, all leaders have two things they provide: faith and definiteness. They have enough strong traits, from whatever combination of strengths, to accomplish what they set out to do. They expect criticism, knowing they are are "damned if they do, and damned if they don't." They keep going in spite of the strength of the opposition and even the jealousy of some on their own team.

All this takes some strong qualities, including; courage, showmanship, a just or narrow tolerance, comprehension, forcefulness, energy, analyticalness and self-reliance. The physical indicators are a broad face, and eyes that are not set too far apart.

If you are associating with people high on leadership:

1. Get them on your projects.
2. Expect them to take over or try to take over.
3. Hold your own ground (as best you can).

If you're with someone lacking in leadership:

1. Give them projects in small chunks.
2. Don't promote them beyond demonstrated capacity.
3. If they show signs of wanting to develop leadership, encourage them. Leadership can be developed or expanded because a number of the traits involved can be strengthened and consciously employed to capacity.

Five
Profile Traits

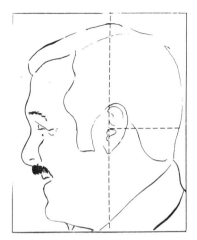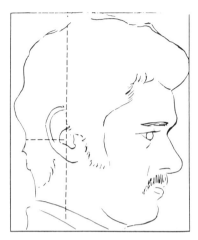

Showmanship

Forward balance Backward balance

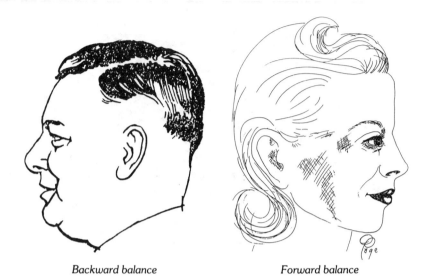

Backward balance   Forward balance

FORWARD-BALANCE OR BACKWARD-BALANCE

Einsetin said, "Everything is relative." This is true of all of our natural human traits. We all have the qualities which make us human, but in different degrees.

One of the most powerful examples of this is how much showmanship or grandstanding we are prone to. We all possess this trait to some degree, but some people are live-wires all the time — "the life of the party." Others, seldom perk up. They are more of the "still-water-runs-deep" type. And, there are those in the middle, who only sparkle and shine if the occasion is special.

Most people have more head in front of the ear opening than behind it. But, the forward-balance individual — the person who is constantly aware of how he or she looks in a situation, and who thrives on constant appreciation and attention — has more than the usual amount, compared to other people. This is the individual who will work hard if shown attention, but is deeply hurt by any kind of criticism. They are apprehensive and uneasy until they sense approval.

In contrast, the individual with less-than-usual forward head balance (as viewed from the side), is more solid, quiet, and steady — more of a "rock of Gibraltar." Whether complimented or not, he or she will do their job.

The forward-balance thinks: "How do I look in the situation?" "What do people think of me?" What is coming up next?" The backward-balance person thinks in terms of the past — who has backed him or her up, who has let them down, what has been accomplished and what has not worked.

Thinking so much in terms of the past, the backward- balance person makes either a good friend or a bitter enemy. He or she is inclined to think about what should have been aid or done after the fact, and is heavy on self-recrimination.

What to do if around a forward-balance person:

1. Compliment frequently and never ignore them. Praise pays off.
2. NEVER criticize unless it's your job to do so. And then, be careful not to do it in front of others unless you have no other choice — this is the individual who feels crucified at losing face.
3. Expect temperamental behavior. This person can blow up, but then gets it out of their system and quickly forgives.

If around a backward-balance person:

1. Talk about old times and pleasant memories.
2. If selling, talk about performance record rather than prestige.
3. Watch out for any old grudges and clear them up. This is the person who puts up with a lot, but blows up when "the straw beaks the camel's back."

Subjective thinker   *Objective thinker*

OBJECTIVE OR SUBJECTIVE THINKING

Quick-witted, wise-cracking people, like the clever Victor Borge or the inimitable Groucho Marx, are built with foreheads that have a steep backward slant when seen in profile. They are mentally quick, but are more on the practical side. They have a gift for communication and in transportation. In debate, they are quick to rebut.

Reciprocally, men and women (or children) with more of a vertical forehead take more time to think things through. They like to learn things in sequence — understanding every phase. Once they grasp the concept, they can speed up and it's like music. Also, they tend to be philosophical, like Socrates, and are interested in the theory more than in the application. They are more sequential and subjective in their thinking.

If you are with the objective, "fast" thinker:

1. Talk about the practical side of the situation.
2. Talk about application rather than theory — get to the point.
3. Expect the other person to jump to conclusions or to think he or she knows what you mean before you finish.

If you are dealing with the sequential, more subjective individual:

1. Explain it step-wise the first time around.
2. Tell them ahead of time so they can get a good running start at it (mention to them Monday that you want it done by Thursday).
3. Don't expect them to jump through the hoop. Give them time to get under way. (This also applies to lovemaking.)

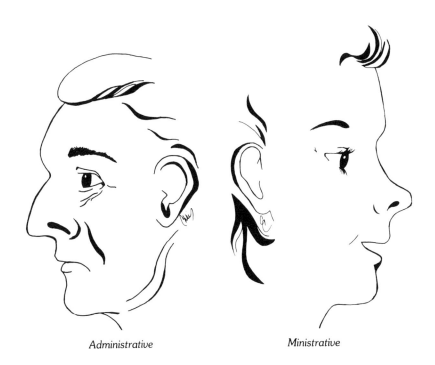

Administrative   *Ministrative*

"Helpful Henrietta"

ADMINISTRATIVE/MINISTRATIVE

The Chinese have a proverb — "watch out for the hawk-nosed person because he is going to look out for himself." This is not necessarily so because each individual possesses more than 60 additional traits. But, other traits being equal, those with a Roman, or hawk nose, have more of a knack for business and feel for administration. They know, all too well, that money does not grow on trees. They can set policy and carry it out.

Commercial-minded individuals, those with the aristocratic, convex nose, like to pay their own way and not be under obligation. Morale is up when more money is coming in than is going out. Bargains are hard to pass by.

Opposite in build, is the ministrative, spontaneously helpful individual with the concave, or "ski jump," nose. Here is someone with a "Mary Poppins" attitude; thinking from the of the other person's perspective and glad to help. This is someone who naturally fits into the service professions.

The Roman-nosed person can be helpful too, as a matter of love or policy — but either has to watch out or look business-like doing it so that their spouse says, "I'm sorry to be putting you out." (This even applies to lovemaking.)

Anyone having what is commonly called a "nose job," should be careful of the genetic make-up of the face. Not any shape of nose will fit on any face. Nature builds in harmony. If Julie Andrews and Barbara Streisand switched noses, each would look odd. The same with Bob Hope and Frank Sinatra.

What to do with someone who is on the administrative side:

1. Pay your own way.
2. Ask where the bargains are.
3. Ask for advice on finances and policy.

What to do around someone with the ministrative build:

1. Tell them your needs.
2. Let them be of service. Say, "I need your help."
3. If you are employing, put them in a helping position.

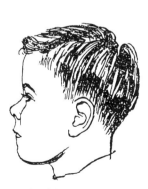

Credulity, too trusting

Incredulous, hard to convince

Credulity

CREDULITY VERSUS SKEPTICISM

When a person has a "nose job" to trade in a businesslike nose for a concave one, part of the change involves turning up the bottom of the nose. As the bottom of the nose leaves the upper lip, it slants upward toward the tip of the nose.

This upward slant of the nose lip, correlates with credulity or open-mindedness, and gives its possessor more of a trusting, juvenile look.

In contrast, many individuals have a downward slant of the bottom of the nose as it goes from lip to tip. This correlates to incredulity and skepticism. This is the individual from Missouri who has to be shown. People built this way have to prove things for themselves. They are born researchers and have to root down to the bottom things.

What do you do when dealing with people with these contrasting dispositions?

If you're dealing with a naturally credulous person:

1. You can safely introduce new ideas.
2. Expect them to believe the first person that tells them something.
3. Be doubtful of the wonderful new things or people they have heard about. Ask them to report back first on how it actually turns out.

If you are dealing with a skeptical person:

1. Expect disbelief.
2. Be ready to prove, especially by demonstration.
3. Keep your dearest ideas to yourself.

*   *   *   *   *

Deep appreciation for music

Sound and music appreciation

SOUND AND
MUSIC APPRECIATION

In a way, the ear functions like a trumpet by funnelling in sound. The rounder the ear, especially the outer perimeter, the more appreciative the person is to sounds, especially music.

Please note that we are speaking of appreciation, not production. Whether an individual has hand dexterity sufficient to master the violin, or a beautiful singing voice, depends upon other factors.

But, you will notice that people with round ears, especially the upper part, have a real love of music. This is more pronounced if they are esthetic (indicated by flat eyebrows).

The type of music they prefer depends upon their taste and individual makeup. As Harry James said about "good" music, "If YOU like it, it's good music."

The idealistic, emotional person likes sentimental music. The hard, rugged person wants loud music.

While watching Montevani's orchestra perform in San Francisco, I noticed that there is a functional similarity between the shape of the ear and the instrument played. Trumpet players had ears which cupped outward. Timpani players had ears with a flat section inside the rim like the flat drum top.

Art and music are areas of obvious native talents. It is hard indeed to try to drill native talent into someone — either they have it or they don't. A devoted music teacher truly loves to find someone with native talent, and help them to develop it. The possessor of such talent owes it to the world to express and share their gift.

But, if your child lacks a gift in this area, don't waste money or create difficulties by being like the father who glowered at the piano teacher about his son; "What do you mean, no talent. TEACH him talent!" It just doesn't work that way. The child has other talents, push those.

Since this book emphasizes how each person is naturally and genetically unique, from now on, take pride in your OWN taste in music. Don't pay attention any longer to what other individuals think you should like (whether rock or classical). Just enjoy your own taste.

Now, you know how to account for people's varying tastes — "to each his own." That's why Baskin Robbins ice cream stores have 31 different flavors!

What to do if you have a deep appreciation of music:

1. Enjoy your own kind — even if you have to wear earphones to do it! Produce music too, if you can. At least sing in the shower!
2. You do everything better to music, so wake up to it, have it as background at your work, if possible, reward yourself with it and lift your spirits with it.
3. Find associates who like YOUR kind of music.

If you're around another music lover:

1. Respect their taste. Draw them out about their preferences. Keep their love of music in mind when buying them gifts — give them an album, for instance.
2. If your tastes are the same, listen to music together, dance with them, go to concerts with them, and join with them in playing music.
3. Have their kind of music as background when entertaining or traveling with them.

Should you happen to be around someone who does not particularly care about music, then get him or her to talk instead about that in which they are interested — hobbies or loved ones — and watch them brighten up.

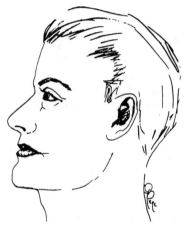

Tenacity, high

TENACITY

Have you ever noticed that a driver who is determined to take the right of way and go through a traffic intersection will set his or her jaw and barrel on through?

Some people are this way all the time — leading with their chin. Once they are involved in an action requiring movement, they will carry through. It is difficult to think of a boxer with a weak chin.

The physical indication for the trait of tenacity is a chin that protrudes noticeably compared to most people. (It is best viewed from the side.) Personality-wise, individuals built this way will also "stick out their chin" for what they think is right. A good prototype is President Theodore Roosevelt.

This trait is minor when compared to traits such as tolerance and self-confidence, but it can be a key in certain situations.

What to do around the tenacious:

1. Let them have the right of way.

2. Anticipate that, once involved, they are the ones more liable to carry through with immediate action.

3. Remember that sometimes they will hang on long after they should let go.

What to do around the un-tenacious:

1. Expect them to give up more quickly.

2. Remember that you are dealing with someone more tractable.

3. Expect them to be less fervent in standing up for what they believe is right.

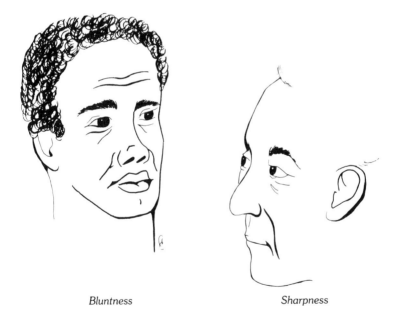

Bluntness   *Sharpness*

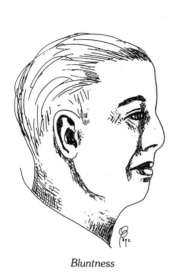

Bluntness

Sharpness

BLUNT OR SHARP

Think of people you know. Those built with a streamlined profile, act streamlined. They are sharp as a tack and are quickly on top of things. They don't miss anything. Hawkshaw, the detective, and Sherlock Holmes are good examples.

On the other hand, think of people you know who are blunt in profile. They are the ones who seldom volunteer their opinion, but speak out plainly when asked. They are blunt in their pronouncements. They are more solid and steady. They take their time in making decisions, but once made, they are "carved in granite." For a prototype, think of actor Glenn Ford, cast in a television series as the solid New Mexico sheriff who takes his time but never veers from his course.

If you are with someone sharp and streamlined:

1. Gear yourself to match their quick wit and observations.
2. Expect to be quickly sized up and observed.
3. Quicken your tempo.

If you are with someone blunt:

1. Expect them to be blunt in speech and action.
2. Remember that they usually will not volunteer an opinion unless solicited, and then they will state it plainly.
3. Give them time to make up their mind, and remember that their mind, once made up, is going to stay made up.

Physicalness—High (left), Low (right)

PHYSICALNESS

Everyone is interested in this trait and tends to remember it because it appears to have some connection with the sex drive; or at least, with initiating sex. People built this way do seem to have more interest in the opposite sex and in everything that represents masculinity or femininity, as the case may be. The general propensity of this trait is just to express one's self physically in an active way, and especially in aerobic manners. It can be in sports or dance.

The structural indicator is a large proportion or fullness at the bottom back part of the head, just above the neck. Often, this is completely hidden by hair or hairstyle. If there is no noticeable development, the score is low and arousal of their interest takes longer. And, like any other trait, it may vary from one side to the other (in which case, the individual may be more interested in physical expression in one mood than in another).

Special Note: Remember that there are scores of other traits also functioning, and thus, the physical propulsion by itself does not mean that the person is constantly in the mood for physical expression, or is always "meat on the table." Other traits, and the total personality, including values and ethics, must be respected.

Points to remember if this trait is prominent:

1. Suggest and encourage wholesome outlets for this trait, such as sports, dancing, physical fitness, hiking, bowling and swimming.
2. Give presents that are distinctly masculine or feminine, as the case may be.
3. If this is your lover, remember you still have to respect the other traits that are pronounced in order for them to express their full potential.
4. If this is your child, encourage participation in sports, hobbies and studies. Keep that child away from dangerous companions.

Points to remember if the trait is not prominent:

1. Expect less interest in the outright physical and more interest in the artistic and esoteric.
2. Provide them with more rest and comfort.
3. If this is you lover, approach more slowly and with love and preparation. Remember the French saying, "There are no frigid wives, just clumsy husbands." After arousal, and with decision to participate, they have just as many nerve endings there as anyone else.

Six
Famous Faces

Eyebrows close to the eyes indicate an affable nature — friends are easily made. This was one reason no man was a stranger to **Mark Twain.**

Notice the white showing under the iris (colored membrane) of **Adolf Hitler's** eye. This indicates great strain, melancholy and unresolved problems.

One reason **Queen Victoria** appears unapproachable in this
drawing is that her eyebrows sit high over her eyes. This indicates
reserve.

When there is an unusually large proportion of head above the eyes,
and an unusually small amount of face under the nose, the individual
is more inclined to mental activity. **William Shakespeare** is a
good example.

Beverly Sills' large, luminous eyes indicate warmth and spirit. In addition, many female singers have a full-budding upper lip.

Full-lipped people are more inclined to verbal and vocal expression. **Mick Jagger** combines his gift for vocal expression with his feel for music.

When the eyes are cold and threatening, you had better beware, as illustrated in this drawing of **King Henry VIII.** The eyes are the best single gauge to an individual.

As with **Winston Churchill,** the strong, wide, firmly-set jaw indicates a determined, commanding nature. It's called the "admiral's jaw."

In face language, people who stick out their chin are tenacious.
Josef Stalin is a good example.

Deep-set eyes indicate serious-mindedness. This type of eye was
very helpful to actor **Bela Lugosi** who played the infamous Count
Dracula. Lugosi had the gift of adding a glassy glitter to the eyes.

People with a sharply slanted, streamlined profile are quick-witted and have an uncanny ability to ad-lib. **Groucho Marx** is a prime example.

Seven

My Vienna Guide

If you know personology, there are no strangers. Even when you're in a foreign country.

On one of our recent European trips, my wife and I were at a streetcar stop in Vienna. I wanted to know how to get to the park where the Strauss concert takes place each afternoon.

Which of the cluster of people at the trolley stop should I ask? Which would naturally WANT to be of help?

Spontaneous helpfulness, being glad to be of assistance (the "Mary Poppins" disposition), is indicated by the concave, retrousse nose). So, knowing a little German, I went up to the lady with the most pronounced "ski-jump" nose in the group. She brightly responded in perfect English, that she would be happy to take us there, and in fact was on her way to the concert herself!

It turned out she had come to Vienna originally as an English "nannie," governess for the children of a diplomat, and had been so taken with this very special city that she made it her permanent home.

Not only did she escort us to the concert, but she went with us afterward to make sure we found the particular restaurant we wanted in the ancient city hall. She declined our invitation to be our dinner guest.

"Do you have a good place to stay tonight?" she asked at the restaurant door, before departing. She was gratified to know we had.

In a way, by knowing personology, you do know the foreign language wherever you go — the language of the face!

Eight

The "Cat Feathers" Expression

There was a young husband who used to park his vehicle beside the bay and contemplate suicide. It was seven years since his wife had given him sex. He didn't feel he was much of a man, or much in her eyes.

A friend told him about personology and he brought his wife in with him for personology analyses.

I made his personology chart and interpreted it. I told him that by nature he was short on self-confidence (then we called it ego,) and that he needed to build more confidence in himself and to be more masterful and courageous.

Meanwhile Elizabeth Whiteside was measuring and counseling his wife, including explaining to her what to do about a pronounced natural trend of stubbornness. The young woman's natural stubbornness was amplified by having had a difficult time in giving birth to their one child.

Then their natural builds were explained to each other.

In those early days of doing personology full-time, I seldom suggested a follow-up counseling, because of the terrific results which come from just the explanation of one's natural makeup and how best to express it.

But this time, I thought, "Seven years without sex. Wow! That's a long 'cold war.' I'd better advise a follow-up." So I asked them to come back a week later for a second session.

When they came down the hallway of my San francisco office suite the next Saturday morning, sweethearts hand in hand, I could see from the husband's expression on his face that he had met with success in making love, and restoring his feeling of manhood.

His expression reminded me of the saying about "cat feathers," describing the appearance of the cat with feathers on his whiskers, who had finally gotten to feast on the family canary which he had been eyeing for so long.

Of course, the restoration of love-making meant more to the husband (and to his mate) than the actual sexual relief. A cold war was over. Harmony and love were back.

With a couple, a good deal of the battle already is won when they both agree to come in for help. And the personology help is so quick, specific, usable and wholesome.

There are three stages in solving any situation.

First, to admit intellectually that the problem exists.

Second, to accept emotionally that something has to be done about it.

Third, to take constructive action.

Both young people had done these three things.

Nine

There's a Place for Everyone

Even animals have face language. Particularly monkeys, and dogs.

But cattle, also. Have you ever been around a slaughterhouse and seen steers killed? — the steers seem to sense and smell death, and try to balk at being led up the ramp into the building. Of course it is humane killing, a pistol shot between the eyes...but it takes a certain cast of personality for a man to hold down a job doing this. (Or even to skin the hides from the still warm bodies and start cutting up the meat.) To do this necessary job in our civilization bothers some individuals less than others, however.

I recall a salesman who had little beady eyes and tight, thin lips, unusual for a salesman because those features indicate a low score on affection and compassion and on outpouring of speech and emotion. Also he had a ruthless streak.

He was having trouble in his marriage. He was dispassionate and matter of fact, but his wife had the opposite build. Her large eyes and full lips indicated her warm and giving nature, naturally demonstrative. She needed a lot of love, openly shown. Even the tone of voice meant much to her. And their small children were much like their mother in needing affection.

Explaining their difference in traits helped save the marriage for man and wife. He now understood her needs. And she gave him extra credit for being more affectionate and demonstrative, now knowing that was not his nature.

Vocationally, there is a place for everyone. I suggested he secure work in connection with a slaughter-house. This he did, and eventually moved up successfully in the meat packing industry.

Conversely, I recall a man who had an affectionate and sympathetic disposition, who had taken a job collecting for the Internal Revenue Service. He had too much compassion for this job. It tore him up to have to crack down on people he found he felt sorry for on meeting them in person. His doctor sent him in for a personological profile.

Previously, this unhappy collector had a secure job he enjoyed, as a postal clerk, serving people face to face. But a relative had persuaded him to change work, saying he would make more money with the IRS.

"Could you get your old job back?" I asked him.

"Maybe I could," he answered, "I've been away from it such a short time." And that's the way it worked out. He even retained his experience rating with the postal service.

To each, his own.

Ten

"Aren't You Psychic?"

Recently I was guest speaker to a business group. The members smiled and nodded in agreement as I spot-analyzed persons they knew, but who were strangers to me.

I had explained personology at the beginning — that each person has a unique inborn disposition and talents, which to a large degree is evidenced in his or her build, particularly in the face.

Still someone asked, "How did you do all that?"

"You saw how I did it," I responded, "I just look at their structure. No need for questions or anything else."

"Yes, but aren't you psychic or something?"

"No, I'm not psychic. And I would hate to try it without personology," was my comment.

The advance of science, particularly of genetics and brain research, has been showing more and more why personology works.

There was a time when there was a leading theory that no one was born with individuality — that we were all born "tabla rasa" (blank tablet,) and were shaped up by whatever happened to us from the outside. Some people held almost as an article of faith, that there was no inborn personality or difference.

Nobody lived that way, of course. Even children in the same family were different. One was artistic, another athletic, another musical one had a knack for business. One had a temper — the others didn't. All ended up following their own tastes and dispositions.

Now it's beginning to be more recognized that inborn qualities play a large — and probably major part — in human individuality...and that the game of lie is best directing our nature, from the inside. When this is done, and we have a good environment also, then we have the best of two worlds.

So personology is now more of the "in" thing. The mainstream of the times is more toward individualism.

Actually, individuality always has been a main issue in humanity's progress. For centuries the swing has been away from being owned or regimented or determined by others — and toward the dignity and freedom of the INDIVIDUAL, to express his or her own talents and nature in their own way, so long as they bothered no one else.

Eleven

The Lonesome Hearts Club

Match-making. Putting people together for dates...presumably lonesome persons happily finding a worthwhile partner with whom to pair off permanently.

Here was a wonderful place for reading people's natural dispositions and seeing who would fit together! This I did on occasion as consultant for a San Francisco lonesome hearts club.

No problem seeing personologically who would click best with whom, from those available. And the larger the number screened, the greater the likelihood of finding good matches.

These people needed help. It was not that they were unattractive or unappealing as persons. Usually they had traits by which they were inclined to hang back...or undersell themselves...or were inclined to be distant or reserved. They profited by coaching on these traits, to better put themselves forward, and to value themselves more.

Few had actual handicaps. One stuttered. But, I told him, a lot of famous people have stuttered — it bothers the stutterer more than it does the other person. And it can be outgrown.

Lonely, heart-empty women had to be warned or protected from "wolves" who would be after them for a night of sex in exchange for a dinner on first date.

One thing I realized from putting persons together in order to get acquainted is that there is a "chemistry" involved...a "chemistry" from the totality of each person.

In each individual, the total is greater than the sum of the parts.

There is that mysterious "chemistry" by which, out of a whole group, one special woman will attract a particular man, another woman won't. For every Jack, there is a Jill.

— The Long-Range Picture—

People have asked me, "Have you ever told two people that they should not marry each other?"

I do not tell people whether they should get married or not. I do not tell people their decisions.

I tell them their natural dispositions in detail, and the particular traits to bear in mind and work on to keep one another happy.

Only once has this prevented a couple from getting married. They decided that would be too much adjusting to do. The girl burst out weeping and cried, "Oh, I knew it all the time — we've been arguing and fighting so much!"

— There <u>Is</u> Such a Thing as Love —

But the big, "mystique" is LOVE. It transcends everything. You can't start it, and you can't stop it. It just happens!

And it's not a matter of reason. It's a matter of the heart...and perhaps even of the spirit. It ennobles.

But for a couple to keep love as the unmatched dream it started out to be, certainly Cupid certainly can stand a little help in each partner understanding the other's unique natural dispositions and needs.

Twelve

The Total Person

Everyone is made up of many qualities. All these facets of human nature combine to form the essence of the individual. But, the thing to remember is that usually there's just one key trait "carrying the ball" in the daily life situations.

Occasionally, two traits have a tug-of-war until one wins. Example: The girl being petted who tells her boyfriend, "Stop it...I love it." Her idealism tells her to wait until they're married, while her physicalness says to go ahead.

Often, two traits can have a booster effect of each other; such as a flare for the dramatic adding style to the showmanship of the forward-balance individual.

But, most of the time, it is a single-shot situation — you will enjoy the effectiveness of talking to the obvious key trait of the individual in front of you. (You can work on your own key trait too if you want — and, in a way, you will find yourself doing this in order to individualize with the other person.)

Talking to even just one key trait allows you to break through that "wall" between you and the other person, and to treat him or her as a special, unique individual. You will have a different look in your eyes and a more friendly tone of voice. You are, therefore, more effective.

Thirteen

For That Something Missing in Your Life

Have you felt that there has been something missing in your life? That somehow, hard as you have tried, that you should have more happiness, be closer to your dear ones, click better at work? That you have only had half of what you needed to know to make things happen right in your individual efforts?

If so, that missing part could well be, to have your own personology analysis done. To understand your own behavioral genetics. Your own individuality, as the special unique individual you are. And how to be your best self. No longer to approach life's daily situations as a generality.

Here are some representative comments of people who have enjoyed the benefits of having their personological chart done:

"If I hadn't had personology, I wouldn't be still married." — M.H., El Paso, Texas.

"Personology is a tool that people can use right away for self-improvement...and for making a better world to live in for themselves and their loved ones.
"The point is that all the positive-thinking self-help courses are only one-half of the loaf — but with personology we have a tailored approach to suit the <u>individual character</u>...knowing which traits to focus on precisely to use one's God-given gifts and make up any deficit." — M.V., Koloa, Hawaii. "The trait-by-trait approach is easier to apply."

"You told me so many helpful things." — G.W. Gold River, California. "The work and activities you said I could do, I have done."

"Thanks for sharing your wisdom. Our marriage received a real blessing that day and a <u>life raft</u>." — L.M., Detroit, Michigan.

"Personology did change my life when I needed it most." — A.H., Livingston, Montana.

"I was stressed out at 15 with the world's problems all

seemingly on my little shoulders. You, personology, and what I could remember from my parents, told me I was O.K. I hung in there and I am so glad I did." — F.A., San Rafael, California

"Getting to know one's self is a life-time goal. Personology has helped. It has benefited me very much." — L.E., Alberta, Canada

"I want to thank you again for the insight we received in personology. It has been so helpful to us individually and as a couple. The tapes are so helpful and have been a tremendous boost to me many times. We both were amazed at what you knew only by looking at us." — J.D., San Diego, California.

"I used personology so much in my Beauty School when I had it. And it's been a God-send when it comes to my children and my husband. I'm forever indebted to you!" — J.K., Vacaville, California.

"I am constantly grateful to you for introducing me to personology. After some 37 years I still find that it smooths the way to my personal relationships as nothing else has." — C.S., Hillsborough, California.

"Personology not only enriched my life, but the lives of my children, grandchildren, and friends." — A.R., Salt Lake City, Utah.

"My 75 years have been happy, healthy and prosperous because of a brief, two-hour introduction to personology with you in 1946...best investment I ever made." — C.M., Rohnert Park, California.

Having your own personology analysis done is like having a birthday — and you are coached on how to direct your particular equipment of traits to get what you want out of life.

Some further examples of how using this knowledge is of benefit:

A couple who had been talking divorce got back together for

keeps. Her words, "Now we have the melody back."

A man who had failed at selling insurance was told that he was built to be a restaurant owner, and became wealthy in that field of business.

A high school boy who was having trouble in his studies was coached personologically and became so good in his studies that he was granted permission to build a computer in the school.

A man who had been on the same job for 13 years without a promotion, was in charge of the whole operation within four years.

A father and daughter who had been unable to communicate got quickly onto good terms together.

Not only can you gain by having your own analysis done, but if you wish to understand other people better from the way they are naturally built, you can do that also. There are tapes and study courses, with classes in various states.

An opera singer who learned personology said, "It took the hurt out of what other people did."

A real estate salesman earned twice as much the next year.

When asked how personology helped him the most, a police chief answered, "Getting confessions."

If you would like your analysis done personally by the author, contact him via Personology Institute of Maui, telephone (808) 572-9613, or 191 Alohilani Street, Post Office Box 304, Pukalani, Hawaii 96788-0304.

For information on study courses, and video and audio tapes, contact the central Personology Institute, 9206 Madison Green Lane, No. 34, Orangevale, California 95662; (916) 988-2614.